Slide and Slurp, Scratch and Burp

More about Verbs

To Isabella
—B.P.C.

Slide and Slurp, Scratch and Burp

More about Verbs

by Brian P. Cleary

illustrated by Brian Gable

M MILLBROOK PRESS / MINNEAPOLIS

Verbs are words like

sneak and sniff,

sneeze and seize

and wheeze and whiff.

4

You might be exploring
the Alps or the Amazon,
maybe restoring
the chair that your grandma's on,

They tell us of horses

that nuzzle and nip,

of bears as they guzzle

and birds as they sip.

They tell us of scooters
both swerving
and stopping,

throws that are curving
or sliding or dropping.

So wrap a package, tie a knot,

clap your hands, or cry a lot.

Triumph, tremble,

trot, and trample,

you'll use a **Verb** for each example!

Fly to the flower shop,
dash to the dance,

swing by the swimming pool,
frolic in France.

Soar to the circus and float to the fair.

Without verbs, your sentence can't go anywhere.

Each sentence **has** a subject—
it's kind of like the star.

It's what the whole thing's all about:

Dave's dish,

Mom's look,

Todd's car.

and lanterns light
and writers write
and clippers cut and trim.

Some **Verbs** aren't the action kind—
They "**link**" instead of "do,"

connecting sentence parts, as in,
"Your dog **appears** quite blue."

These linking verbs
connect a subject
to a word or phrase

that's called a
subject complement.
It's done in lots of ways:

It became ridiculous.

That strudel sure **smells** great.

The crime **remains** a mystery.

This play **seems** second rate.

21

Were and was
work this way, too—
they're forms of "be" as well.

I am Shannon.
He **is** Mort.

Were you the one
who **was** in court?

There **are** times
a form of "**be**"
is all that's needed, verbally.

Whether you slide

or you slip

or you slurp,

if you should scream

or you scratch

or you burp,

if you're **making** a fraction
or **writing** a blurb,

because there **is** action,
you **know** it's a verb.

So if you should gloat

or you glisten

or listen,

Say to the chef,
"Take that out and put this in."

28

whether you pounce

or pronounce

or perturb,

I'm here to announce
that you're using a verb!

So, what IS a Verb?

Do you know?

ABOUT THE AUTHOR & ILLUSTRATOR

BRIAN P. CLEARY is the author of the Words Are Categorical™ and Math Is Categorical™ series, as well as Rainbow Soup: Adventures in Poetry and Rhyme and PUNishment: Adventures in Wordplay. He lives in Cleveland, Ohio.

BRIAN GABLE is the illustrator of many Words Are Categorical™ books, the Math Is Categorical™ series, and the Make Me Laugh! joke books. He lives in Toronto, Ontario, with his wife and two children.

Text copyright © 2007 by Brian P. Cleary
Illustrations copyright © 2007 by Millbrook Press, Inc.

Millbrook Press, Inc.
A division of Lerner Publishing Group
241 First Avenue North
Minneapolis, MN 55401 U.S.A.

Website address: www.lernerbooks.com

Library of Congress Cataloging-in-Publication Data

Cleary, Brian P., 1959—
    Slide and slurp, scratch and burp : more about verbs / by Brian P. Cleary ;
    illustrations by Brian Gable.
        p.   cm. — (Words are categorical)
    ISBN-13: 978-0-8225-6207-8 (lib. bdg. : alk. paper)
    ISBN-10: 0-8225-6207-3 (lib. bdg. : alk. paper)
    1. English language—Verb—Juvenile literature. I. Gable, Brian, 1949— ill.
    II. Title. III. Series: Cleary, Brian P., 1959— Words are categorical.
PE1271.C57 2007
428.2—dc22   2006012096

Manufactured in the United States of America
1 2 3 4 5 6 - JR - 12 11 10 09 08 07